The Financial Feminism Guide

On How to Master Your Money
and Live the Life You Want

by

Thelma D. Johnson

Table of contents

Introduction

In a world in which making financial decisions can frequently appear scary and difficult, there is a growing movement that is transforming the face of personal finance. This movement is known as Financial Feminism. It is a movement with the goal of enabling people of all genders to take charge of their financial destinies, liberate themselves from the constraints that have traditionally been placed on them based on their gender, and build a life that is characterized by financial freedom and abundance.

In the pages that follow, we will get started on a journey that will change the way you think by challenging traditional ideas about money, equality, and self-determination. This book is not simply about money; rather, it serves as a rallying cry for people of all walks of life to accept the tenets of financial feminism and take charge of their own financial destinies.

It is not the goal of financial feminism to exclude anyone; rather, it is a movement that acknowledges the right of all people, regardless of gender, to have equal access to the resources, information, and opportunities that are necessary to prosper in today's world. It is a movement that recognises the systematic biases and inequities that exist in our financial institutions and gives a path for dismantling those biases and inequalities.

Chapter 1

The Feelings Amid Money

When it comes to money, people are more logical. We don't make and stick to a budget or save money every pay period, even though it would be in our best interests to do so. We know we need a financial plan, but we put it off, and it never gets done. We either spend too little out of shame or too much out of carelessness. We often feel ashamed of how we handle money.

It's important to consider how your connection with money is nuanced. Your money (and, more generally, your finances) are a complex of informational elements, problems, and possibilities you think about, deal with, and feel strongly about. Your financial condition is impacted by your decisions, affecting your thoughts and subsequent actions. Additionally, the relationship develops over a lifetime.

These are the three most important things to understand regarding the psychology of our relationships with money:

- Emotions are crucial.

- A vicious loop between avoidance and anxiety exists.
- You psychologically can't completely get away from your family and your past.

Money and feelings

The four emotions that matter most regarding money are fear, guilt, shame, and envy. It's worthwhile to put some effort into becoming aware of the emotions that are particularly associated with money for you since, without awareness, they will frequently take precedence over reason and influence your behavior.

What is there to fear, exactly? As many different storylines exist, there are potential outcomes. The fear of running out, the fear of looking foolish, the fear of inspiring jealousy, and the fear of being exposed or humiliated are all prevalent worries.

Shame and guilt are two different emotions. Hurting others makes you feel guilty, whereas letting yourself down or failing to uphold your standards of right and wrong makes you feel ashamed.
You may feel bad if you have more than your friends, have not been charitable, or have too much money.
One of the most prevalent and potent emotions connected to money and personal economics is shame. It is a significant factor in why people refrain from acting upon advice. It makes sense to want to keep your humiliation from being brought to light.

Here are just a few examples of how one could feel ashamed about having money:

- I need the necessary funds.

- I've refrained from considering money.
- I've avoided making the financial preparations I should have made (a safety net, retirement planning, and prudent budgeting).
- I know absolutely nothing about this.
- I need to spend more.
- I spend money when I'm depressed.

A vicious cycle is produced when avoidance and shame interact. When you're overcome with guilt, your natural inclination is to avoid everything that makes you uncomfortable. Even more shame and avoidance result from that avoidance. The next thing you know, your taxes are past due, and six years have passed since you decided to schedule an appointment with a financial planner, but nothing has transpired.

People who put off taking care of financial obligations frequently accuse themselves of procrastination and believe they are simply lazy or lack discipline. That is unhelpful, judgmental, and derogatory. What we typically refer to as procrastination is the psychological mechanics of avoidance. We must use various avoidance strategies when faced with anything that causes fear or discomfort. The problem is that avoidance helps lower anxiety in the near term. You're more likely to do it again in the same situation because it worked the first time.

This is how it happens. You're considering sitting down, closely examining your finances, and developing a practical financial strategy. However, even the thought of it causes you to worry because you fear you won't be able to accept that, for instance, you don't have nearly enough money saved for your children's school. Avoidance results from this anxiety. You put it off and divert your attention. Your anxiety level immediately decreases at that point, reinforcing your decision to avoid it. You keep going through this loop. However, each momentary decrease in anxiety doesn't exactly return you to your pre-anxiety baseline. Your total degree of anxiety also keeps rising over time.

Compare this pattern to having to complete a dreaded task. You feel momentarily more anxious as you face the truth. But if you stick with it, your overall worry will gradually decrease. To gain from the long-term reduction in anxiety, you must be willing to accept that momentary rise in distress. The lesson learned is that reality is always your friend.

Other money-related feelings include hostility, greed, excessive excitement, and the social psychology phenomenon "jumping on the bandwagon." Some of these are more pertinent to professional investing than to personal finance, for example.

Chapter 2

Expenditures

You must approach saving money appropriately if you want to do it. Saving money for the future is necessary, but how can you ensure it will stick? You might encounter problems if you don't have a plan and some excellent ideas. To reduce your spending, adhere to these easy suggestions.

1. Make savings objectives

Planning is usually a brilliant idea. Are you putting money aside to purchase a car? Perhaps all you want to do is reduce your credit card debt. Whatever the situation, make goals. You will be ready to work toward that objective once you know what you are saving for. Consider your goals as a layer of protection, keeping you from overspending.

2. Create a Budget

Observe your expenditures and record everyday transactions in a budget spreadsheet. You will eventually see how much money you spend each day, week, month, and year. You can use a search engine to uncover a variety of reliable budget planners if you need assistance. You may examine your spending and identify the areas where your wallet leaks money. Ensure you are spending only what you make by keeping track of your revenue similarly. Eliminate the costs that aren't increasing your savings and observe how your income soars.

3. Have a balance before you spend

Before leaving the house to go out, pay all your debts. You are more prone to spend money carelessly when oblivious to your financial situation. However, clearly understanding your finances will benefit you when you are out and about. Keeping your checkbook in balance will give you the self-control to limit your expenditures.

4. Hold off three days

Wait three days if you are tempted to buy a large item. Consider if you need what you want to buy while waiting. You'll be able to tell if it's something you genuinely want to buy after the initial rush of impulse buying wears off.

5. Eat your meal.
Don't eat in a restaurant. You can find healthier food in your refrigerator, and staying in will save you a ton of money. Before making another trip to the shop, look in your pantry because you also have some food there. In addition, eat something before you go to the store because a hungry consumer will spend more money! Always go to the supermarket after the food has run out. You'll make fewer trips and pay less for groceries, which will enable you to make some savings.

6. Bring lunch.
Numerous people often spend their money at pricey restaurants and food carts.

You can avoid falling into this trap by packing a lunch before you leave for work. By implementing this advice, you'll eat better and save a lot of money.

7. Make a Shopping List

Before you leave the house, make a list of the things you need to buy. Just follow the list, which will energize you while you are out. This makes it simple to steer clear of impulsive purchases. Just keep in mind that nothing on the list may be purchased.

8. Stop sending emails and catalogs

You receive emails and catalogs from retailers frequently. They want you to open them so you can peruse their newest offers, which will captivate you. Avoid opening them! This usually works. Call the businesses that send you catalogs and request that they take your name off their mailing list. You can resist the urge to look at the newest discounts in these methods (and save some of your hard-earned money!).

9. Store your credit cards away
Your credit cards may be your worst enemy when trying to conserve money. As a result, put them somewhere you will need help to get to quickly. A safe is a brilliant place to start because it requires time to input the combination, and the credit card won't be easily accessible. There are other options than safes for stopping credit card use. You can attempt anything to make it more difficult for you to get the card out.

You can take more extreme measures (especially if you don't have a safe). Try burying your cards in the backyard after wrapping them in plastic. They could also be frozen. Put the card in an icebox with a water bowl next to it. (Place a penny on top to prevent the card from floating.) You will have to defrost or dig your credit card back out the next time you need to use it, which are both immensely powerful deterrents.

10. Cut up your cards.
The icebox trick, therefore, failed. Or you're a great digger. Despite your efforts to conceal your credit cards, you used them to make purchases. Chop them up, no problems. Cut up your debit cards if you discover that you are using them excessively. There will be no more impulsive excursions to the ATM or shopping. No credit or debit means you can't use your cards for impulsive purchases.

Chapter 3

The strategy for managing money

Have you thought about what your strategy is for managing your finances? Have you identified them? Reviewing your assets and liabilities, discussing your financial objectives, and taking steps to get you moving in the right direction should all be part of your economic game plan.

Your financial objectives will shape your plan for the next five to ten years. Whether you want to buy a home or prefer to rent one is a decision that must be made. You should budget for a down payment of around 20% of the home's purchasing price when you want to buy a home. Accordingly, you must save $40,000 for a home worth $200,000. You'll also need cash or credit for house improvements, including cosmetic ones like new paint, a kitchen backsplash, or faucets. Determine whether there will be a monthly association fee or any other charges with renting the home if that is your financial aim. These charges could include a parking fee, a maintenance cost, or a pest control fee. Taking action will help you stay on the correct track. To ensure you are implementing them and moving forward, you should evaluate these action steps every three to four months. If your circumstances have changed—perhaps because of a new debt, a child, or another factor—you should check the procedures and see if anything needs to be modified. The actions listed below can help you achieve your financial objectives:

- Analyze your list of possessions and liabilities, then choose a debt repayment strategy. You should consider filing for bankruptcy if your minimum monthly payments are unreasonable. You should make as much monthly payment as possible toward paying off your debt.

- Budget your money. Verify that all of your monthly or no expenses are included in your spending plan. Pet food, medical care, and summer camp costs should all be considered. Choose where you must and want to spend your money. Start setting aside more money for your aspirations and other financial goals the sooner you finish paying off your debt.

- Organize your savings. According to their excellent rule of thumb, 10% of each paycheck should be put into a savings account. Try not to touch any money you receive from bonuses, overtime pay, or tax refunds. Doing this saves you money for unexpected costs like auto or home repairs or unexpected medical expenses. A surprising thing will always occur in life. Make appropriate preparations.

- Don't spend too much money. The ability to purchase a new vehicle every two years may not be possible if your objective is to pay off your mortgage in five years. Put the most crucial things first and keep the other costs minimal. This doesn't exclude you from eating out three times per week, but you can cut back on expenses by skipping cable.

- Build a strong credit history for yourself. Good credit makes low-interest rates on mortgages and auto loans possible. When you have excellent credit, applying for a new credit card may be more accessible.

- When the timing is appropriate, include a significant other. The ideal time to have a significant other in your financial goals is one that you alone can determine. Before a wedding, a discussion of financial objectives should be conducted. It should also happen before opening a joint account or jointly paying bills. An effective plan and open lines of communication will undoubtedly improve a connection.

- Be flexible with your plan's modifications. Your life course will shift several times. Being adaptable is essential. Analyze your financial game plan and evaluate what has to be modified.

Chapter 4

How investing operates.

Investing: What Is It?

Investing is investing money to work overtime on a project or achieve positive returns (earnings that outweigh the initial expenditure). It's allocating resources, typically capital (i.e., money), hoping to make money, making gains, or making a profit.

One can engage in various activities (directly or indirectly), such as utilizing capital to start a business or buying assets like real estate to rent and sell at a profit.

In contrast to saving, investing involves putting money to work, which carries an implied risk that the connected project(s) could fail and cause a financial loss. The other way that investing differs from speculation is that the latter involves wagering on short-term price swings rather than putting the money to work.

A person invests to increase their money over time. The fundamental tenet of investing is the expectation of a favorable return in income or price appreciation with statistical significance. There is a reasonably wide range of assets which one can invest and generate a return.

Different Investments
Most financial instruments used today to raise and invest funds in enterprises are called investments. These businesses then take that capital and put it to work, expanding or making money.

Although there are many different sorts of investments, the following are the most typical ones:

1. Stocks A stock purchase makes the buyer a fractional owner of the company. Shareholders own a company's stock and can benefit from its expansion and success by increasing

the value of their investment and receiving regular dividend payments from the company's earnings.

2. Bonds Bonds are debt obligations issued by organizations like governments, municipalities, and businesses. A bond means that you own a portion of a company's debt and are qualified to receive periodic interest payments as well as the face value of the bond once it matures.

3. Investment managers manage funds, pooled instruments that let investors buy stocks, bonds, preferred shares, commodities, etc. Mutual funds and exchange-traded funds are two of the most popular categories of funds. Exchange traded funds trade on stock exchanges and, like stocks, are regularly valued during the trading day,

unlike mutual funds, which do not trade on a business and are evaluated at the close of the trading day. Fund managers can actively manage Mutual funds and ETFs or track benchmarks like the S&P 500 or the Dow Jones Industrial Average.

4. Alternative Derivatives and Options
Financial instruments known as derivatives get their value from another device, like a stock or index. Popular products like options contracts provide the buyer the choice, but not the duty, to purchase or sell a security at a specified price within a predetermined time window. Leverage is frequently used in derivatives, making them a high-risk, high-reward investment.

5. Commodities

Commodities include metals, oil, grains, and animal goods, along with financial instruments and currencies. Commodity futures are contracts to purchase or sell a specific amount of an item at a given price of a particular future date, or ETFs are the two ways they can be traded. Commodities can be exchanged for speculative or risk-hedging objectives.

Comparing Investment Approaches
Let's contrast a few of the most popular investing approaches:

By actively managing the investment portfolio, active investing seeks to "beat the index" instead of passive investing, which aims to match the market. Contrarily, passive investing promotes a passive strategy, such as purchasing an index fund, as a tacit admission that it is challenging to outperform the market continuously. Both methods have advantages and disadvantages, but only a few fund managers routinely outperform their benchmarks to make active management's higher costs worthwhile.

Value versus growth High-growth companies often have higher valuation ratios like Price-Earnings (P/E) than value companies, which is why growth investors like to invest in them. Value investors search for businesses with PE ratios much lower than growth company ratios and greater dividend yields because these businesses may be temporarily or permanently out of favor with investors.

What to Invest In

Self- Directed Investing

The answer to "how to invest" depends on whether you are a Do-It-Yourself (DIY) investor or would rather have a professional manage your money. Due to the low commissions and simplicity of trading on their platforms, many investors who prefer to handle their funds have accounts at discounts or online brokerages.

DIY investing, also known as self-directed investment, calls for knowledge, expertise, time commitment, and emotional restraint. If you don't fit these descriptions, letting a professional manage your money could be a better idea.

Investing Professionally Managed
Wealth managers typically handle investments for investors who seek professional money management. AUM, or assets under control, is the standard proportion wealth managers charge their clients as their fee. Even though hiring an experienced money manager costs more than managing money alone, some investors are

willing to pay for the ease of having an expert handle the research, investment decisions, and trading.

Robotic investment advice
Some investors decide which investments to make based on advice from computerized financial consultants. Robo-advisors, which use algorithms and artificial intelligence to generate recommendations, compile vital data about the investor and their risk profile. Robo-advisors, which operate with little human intervention, provide services akin to those of a human investment advisor at a lower cost. With technological developments, Robo-advisors can now do more than choose assets. They can aid in the creation of retirement plans as well as the administration of trusts and other retirement accounts like 401(k)s.

Chapter 5

Adopting a financially feminist way of life

Regaining control over your finances, laying a solid foundation, and asserting yourself in the financial world will allow you to live the life you want now and in retirement. The objective is to achieve financial freedom, which enables women to use the money they have earned to make their own decisions.
By enabling women to manage their finances, financial feminism aims to address this issue and others. We already know that women

often earn less than males. However, they may also need more knowledge and assurance to handle their finances, advance their employment, and invest and save money.

Financial literacy begins at a young age, and numerous studies have shown that the gap between boys and girls in allowances begins early and frequently for less work. Those differences persist into maturity.

In a similar role, women still only make 86 cents on a man's dollar, according to the Global Gender Gap Report 2021. In almost every profession, women in the United States make less money than men. Additionally, the pandemic has caused a more than 30-year decline in women's labor force participation, which will likely significantly affect women's collective financial freedom.

In addition, women often live longer than males do. According to German researchers,

75% of women between the ages of 35 and 50 are at risk of living in poverty when they are older because they are not accumulating enough money for retirement.

What is the long and short of it? In addition to having a lower labor market participation rate than males and other structural prejudices, women earn less than their male counterparts. Women are consequently much less likely to make investments and accumulate wealth.

Women's Financial Challenges: Special Issues

When creating a successful financial future for themselves, women confront particular difficulties.

1 Shame

How often have you heard that discussing money is impolite? Or inquire about your coworkers' salaries? Women are brainwashed from a young age to avoid talking about money. They are taught that it is disrespectful to even ask about money. It is a deeply ingrained idea that has misogyny at its core. It is unsurprising that women grow up with shame related to money and finances. But how can women advance if they never discuss money? How can they develop and learn? Only recently have ideas like pay transparency and open conversations about issues like the salary, literacy, and retirement gap begun to gain traction. Changing your viewpoint is the most significant approach to get over this embarrassment in the interim.

2. Lack of comprehension

How often have you initiated a conversation about the stock market with someone (or, more accurately, been drawn into one by someone who claims to be an expert on stocks)? To feel as if you cannot comprehend what the other person is saying? Most individuals aren't taught what terms like "short" and "mutual fund" mean because the stock market has its terminology. Furthermore, financial managers with ulterior motives frequently conceal themselves behind the language to give the impression that investing is beyond your comprehension to feel more important.

What is the first step to feeling more at ease with investment and money? Realizing that, although it could appear frightening or overwhelming, it's much simpler than many of us first believed.

3. Lack of direction

Women get different financial counseling and advice than males, which makes it harder for them to become financially successful in their later years. Most young women need more financial education or support. That implies that they can be presented with more expensive financial products when they consult a financial counselor. More instruction in budgeting and financial investing may also be needed.

Why is it necessary for women to be financially independent?

You have much more control over your life choices when you handle your finances and plan for the future. Do you intend to become pregnant? Do you want to spend five years traveling? Will you concentrate on your career? Do you desire EVERYONE of these things? Your ability to make these decisions for yourself, thanks to your financial situation, can alter the direction of your life. Even though you're married, you don't have to rely on someone else's income if you don't want to.

This is particularly relevant given that men and women continue to experience financial disparity throughout their lives. In addition, while living longer than males, women frequently wind up with lower retirement savings throughout their lives.

How can you take charge of your future finances?

Financial feminism encourages more women to regain control of their finances by educating, empowering, and involving them in this process. How to join the movement is as follows:

1. Be fearless

Having only some of the answers is acceptable. Women routinely do worse than males regarding financial literacy, which affects their capacity to make wiser financial decisions. This means investment, retirement planning, and money accumulation terrify women more than men. The lack of confidence in women can be attributed to one-third of the gender difference in financial literacy, according to research. The report shows that although women are less financially literate than males, they are more knowledgeable.

It all boils down to having confidence and being fearless. How, then, can you increase your trust in the financial sector? Try the following advice:

- Put a little money into the stock market so you can gain experience.

- Teach young people early about financial matters. Having kids makes this very crucial!
- Find out what your friends and family are doing by asking them.
- Ask for expert assistance
- Discuss money
- As I've already said, many people learn early on to steer clear of talking about money, particularly women. That refers to your income, the income of your coworkers, and your budget. The list continues.

Only 14% of women claimed in the Ellevest Financial Wellness Survey 2021 to regularly speak with others when seeking help and guidance. According to nearly half (45%) of women who responded to the same poll, talking about money makes them feel more supported, relieves stress (41%), and increases their confidence in their ability to make sound financial decisions (39%). Talking about money may be challenging, particularly given its stigma and secrecy. It is not typical. For this reason, it's crucial to maintain voicing your opinions and discussing money.

You learn what is and isn't possible when discussing money with your friends, coworkers, family, and spouse.

2. Surround yourself with uplifting people.

You might feel uncomfortable talking to your family or friends just now. That's alright. You may start surrounding yourself with helpful financial role models and instructors immediately, both online and offline. For instance, Tori Dunlap, a social media influencer and the creator of Her First 100K provides online counsel to women to teach them more about positioning themselves for success.

3. At work, speak up.
For a lot of people, financial conversations start at work. The better you can make things in your workplace, the better it will be for all the other women there. Consider campaigning for measures that will benefit women in your office, such as paid parental leave, more excellent vacation time, flexible working rules, and more, if you have a voice at work.
Furthermore, it entails advocating for yourself. It can be challenging to advocate for equal pay with your male colleagues. It's possible that you even experience imposter syndrome. However, bargaining at work can matter.

4. Possess personal accounts

Consider opening your financial accounts, whether single, married, or living with others. While handling your finances, you can still contribute to the household's costs. Owning your budget might benefit your sense of self-worth in an emergency. Maintaining at least one account is crucial, even if your relationship is close.

5. Recognize how you spend your money. Everybody manages their money differently. Many people pick up money management skills by observing their parents or friends. How we learn to manage our finances is greatly influenced by our family's history and experiences.

Building a successful financial future may depend on understanding how you spend your money. For instance, you can take action to control or limit bad habits if you are aware that you overpay on a specific category of spending. You can handle your money more effectively if you know your skills and weaknesses. The trick is to be present. Track your development and determine how you can improve at the month's end.

6. Have personal objectives
No matter their marital status, women should always have their own financial goals. Whether it's paying off your school loans early or saving money for your child's future, your objectives and the goals you share with your spouse can help you advance in life.

Conclusion

As a woman, Investing is a great way to get on the path to financial stability, and you only need a little money to get started. You can enhance your long-term savings outlook with relatively simple actions, such as raising your pension contributions at a younger age. Risk is unavoidable; nevertheless, you can choose the level of risk with which you are most at ease, and investing for the long term helps cushion the impact of any short-term volatility that will undoubtedly occur.

It is reasonable to experience a sense of financial disengagement. Still, your choices today will either hurt or benefit your future self, and the journey toward gaining control of your finances does not have to feel like a source of worry. The goal is to lessen the likelihood of future anxiety attacks while enhancing one's sense of safety and calm. The initial step in achieving financial independence and literacy is all that is required to get started on this journey that will last a lifetime.